A DANCER TO GOD

A DANCER TO GOD

Tributes to

T. S. ELIOT

Ted Hughes

faber and faber

LONDON · BOSTON

First published in 1992
by Faber and Faber Limited
3 Queen Square London WC1N 3AU

Photoset by Wilmaset Ltd, Wirral
Printed in England by Clays Ltd, St Ives plc

'The Death of Saint Narcissus' & 'Humouresque'
are reprinted from
The Complete Poems and Plays of T. S. Eliot
by permission of Faber and Faber

A CIP record for this book
is available from the British Library

ISBN 0–571–16606–7

2 4 6 8 10 9 7 5 3 1

For Valerie Eliot

CONTENTS

I · THE TRULY GREAT

On the Unveiling of the Plaque
to T. S. Eliot
at 3 Kensington Court Gardens, London w8,
on 26 September 1986

Since we are all of one mind, at this gathering, there is little that really needs to be said.

We are here to pay a small and simple tribute to a great poet.

Once I have said that, we realize immediately, I think, that the term 'great poet', so bare and unqualified, is not enough for the man we have come to honour.

Thomas Stearns Eliot, who was born ninety-eight years ago today, in St Louis, in the United States, and who lived here at 3 Kensington Court Gardens from 1957 to the end of his life, was and is much more, to us, than the words 'great poet' can easily denote.

Today is perhaps the right time, and this the right place, to bring to mind just what kind of poet he was.

The term 'great poet' is used too freely. And the variant 'major poet' is abused just as much. We are all aware of this. We know that truly great poets are exceedingly rare. And yet, during my lifetime, I have never heard Thomas Stearns Eliot referred to except as a species on his own, a great poet in an altogether more valuable and separate class of greatness than all those of his contemporaries, in our language, who are also frequently dubbed 'great'. In the latter half of his life, this was never seriously questioned. Somehow the consensus materialized, as if through instinct, among all his colleagues in the poetry of English, that he is not merely a great poet, but, finally, one of that exceedingly rare kind, one of the 'truly great'. And not only one of the truly great, but simply *the* poet of our times. As if there could be only the one.

While he lived, each year that passed consolidated the sovereignty and authority of his position as the poetic master in our tongue. And each year, too, extended the recognition of this fact through other languages and cultures.

Since his death in 1965, what has happened to his greatness?

During the last decade or so, I have repeatedly observed a curious thing. Scattered about the world, at present, there are a number of poets who, in the history of their own languages, have a strong claim to be called 'great', and who are generally acknowledged as such. These are men and women now in their sixties and seventies, and older. They are poets whose work has survived many fashions and crazes, and who have earned their reputations under the most exacting tests that history can impose. They are now old enough to look back over the cataclysm of this century, and to come to some conclusions.

Again and again, in recent years, I have been startled, and delighted, to hear these poets say that after everything, after the extraordinary Babel of revolutions and counter-revolutions in the poetic and spiritual lives of all modern cultures, in all languages, there remains, for them, a supreme spiritual master and a supreme sacred book – a book that more than any other now gathers them into itself as this century heads towards its close. The master is Eliot, and the book – his *Collected Poems*. And especially, within the *Collected Poems*, that crown which he set on his lifetime's effort – *The Four Quartets*.

This election of Eliot to the place of grand master, not

simply of poetry in English but of all the poetries of the modern world, begins to define that term 'great poet', as it applies to him. Or rather, it begins to define what we mean by 'truly great poet'.

One circumstance in this, which might give us pause, is that he did and does share his supremacy in modern English with one other poet – I mean with W. B. Yeats.

It is impossible, and superfluous, for those of us who revere these two inspired men to the limit of our capacity to cast a vote for either one against the other. We are simply grateful to have both. Yet it is clear, too, that though we call them both twentieth-century poets they belong to profoundly different worlds. And by their very differences they define each other.

Yeats was the culmination of specific poetic traditions, the complex of autochthonous traditions in these islands. Though he borrowed some things from elsewhere, it was Yeats's pride that he drew his artistic principles and his visionary strength out of the roots of this old, insular world – a world to which all of us here belong, and which is peculiar to us. But Eliot was the prophet of a new world, and for better and for worse we belong to this one too. And this new world is not at all peculiar to these islands. It is the world which has already, in its soul, and throughout all its peoples, suffered the global holocaust, and must now, somehow, find in its own ashes the spiritual strength to resurrect itself. And it was Eliot's humility to know, with what seemed like knowledge inborn, that nothing matters now but to search for this strength, and to find it. Just as it was his heroic achievement to become the exemplary conscience and voice of this knowledge.

This is the sense in which he is understood, and recognized as their prophet, by the poets of the modern world. In universal significance, in psychological depth, in the humility with which he submits to the revelation, and

5

in the wholeness and power and accuracy of his response to it, he stands in the centre of the cyclone of our modern apocalypse. And he speaks from that centre, as a unique, still point of awareness and eloquence, in our time comparable perhaps only to such a figure as Einstein.

In other words, while Yeats, in all the greatness and great beauty of his work, stays confined within English, Eliot moves at large throughout all variations of language and culture, claimed by all, as they become aware of him, and needed by all.

This, I think, helps to define the essential difference between the 'great' and the 'truly great', between the poetry of a distinctive, albeit compound, national culture and the poetry of this new, unprecedented, psychic simultaneity of all cultures, this sudden, inner confederation of all peoples, subjected as they are, under the tyranny of modern history, to a single spiritual calamity.

The greatness of Yeats, then, sets him among the great national poets, each within the matrix of his or her own culture and language. But what company can we find for this different greatness of Eliot? What other poets, in the past, have spoken with such finality, and so piercingly, in all tongues? They are very, very few. Eliot himself would call them 'Men whom one cannot hope to emulate'. And yet, as I say, those among the world's living poets best qualified to make the election are inclined, more and more, to set him in that succession, among those very, very few, the truly great names in the evolution of world poetry.

To honour a man of this kind, a plaque does seem to be a very small tribute. But we should bear in mind that in this plaque we are acknowledging something else. We are acknowledging that this truly great American paid a great tribute to us. He honoured us by choosing England and this city for his life and labours. In every way he committed himself to us: in his religion, in his secular,

6

cultural allegiance, and finally in his most intimate and personal feelings – in the marriage which brought him happiness in this building.

It rests with us, now, to make sure that these things also are remembered, here in this plaque to Thomas Stearns Eliot.

2 · THE SONG OF SONGS
IN THE VALLEY OF BONES

Introduction
to a reading of *The Waste Land*,
Palace Theatre, London,
25 September 1988

Before we move on to the final part of our programme, I would like to thank all those who have made this evening possible.

For this magnificent space, I would like to thank Andrew Lloyd Webber. Our very special thanks are due to the fairy godmother whose idea this event was, and who has managed and master-minded it right up to this moment, Josephine Hart. And I would like to thank the actors. In particular, on behalf of the Arvon Foundation, I would like to express our gratitude to them all for having given this entire evening free.

The Arvon Foundation began, and continues, mainly as a school for poets. This is not an absolutely new idea. The first colleges in the British Isles, for centuries the only colleges, were colleges for poets. These were the poetic colleges of the ancient Celtic world. Originally they were Druidic or religious colleges – and the old Irish word for the poets they trained was *fili*, which means 'seer'. Tradition dwells on the paranormal, clairvoyant, somewhat magical powers of these individuals. The training lasted twenty-five years, and was phenomenally arduous. But the graduated *fili* was considered second in rank only to the King. Ideally he carried the whole culture of the people. He was the curator and the re-animator of the inner life which

11

held the people together and made them what they were.

Perhaps our actors tonight will be pleased to hear that these poets of the highest order – the *fili* – never recited their own poems. For that they were dependent on another professional – the *reacaire* – the reciter.

The poetic colleges vanished as the old Celtic society crumbled away. Even so, they hung on for a surprisingly long time. The last fully trained *fili* died in the Hebrides – one in South Uist, another in the Isle of Skye – around 1720. Since that time, a flourishing school for poets, even of the humblest sort, the poems of master poets being recited by their *reacaire*, and a noble audience, have never again come together in these islands – until tonight. But the main reason that we are here, on this particular night, is, of course, that we are dedicating this event to the memory of our master of masters, Thomas Stearns Eliot, on the centenary eve of his birth.

Eliot himself was by way of being something of a 'seer' – and a 'seer' of a very rare kind. It is precisely the clairvoyant quality of his vision of contemporary urban reality, the hallucinated depth and complexity and actuality of it, which sets him apart from, and perhaps a little above, all other poets of the last three hundred years.

The poem which presents this vision most fully, most nakedly, is *The Waste Land*. And this is the work we are now going to hear recited by the *reacaire*. Eliot generally refrained from and even disapproved of any introductory comment before the reciting of his own poems. He took pains to let them communicate only in their own terms. But *The Waste Land* is a special case. And fortunately he provided some notes for this work which do give us the wavelength on which we have to listen – for what the poem has to tell us. I will just touch on the main points.

It is possible that more has been written about *The Waste Land* – about the subtleties and implications of it,

the problems and riddles which it poses – than about any
other poem.

· We are often told that coming when it did, in 1922,
out of the shock and exhaustion immediately following
the First World War, this poem stands between the old
world and the new; that it recapitulates the decay and
collapse of the inner life of the old world, and at the
same time divines – and defines – the spiritual condition
which became the cornerstone of the new.

All that seems to be true. It is also true that Eliot
devised totally new poetic procedures to give form to his
revelation.

But the curious fact remains: this immensely learned,
profound, comprehensive, allusive masterpiece is also a
popular poem. And popular with the most unexpected
audiences. I remember when I taught fourteen-year-old
boys in a secondary modern school, of all the poetry
I introduced them to, their favourite was *The Waste
Land*.

It seems to be the case that this notoriously difficult
work is wide open, in some way, to those who can hear it
as a musical composition. The form of the poem is
dominated, even determined, by Eliot's music.

At the surface, this music operates through the
sequence and cadence of words within each line, the
sequence and cadence of lines within each paragraph,
and so on. But at the deepest level too the music is
decisive. The poem is founded in an assemblage of states
of feeling, or rather states of soul, exactly as music is: an
assemblage of human cries.

This makes it also a drama for voices. There are five
sections, and except for the fourth each section is made
up of several short poems, or rather speeches, for different male and female voices.

These voices do not speak to each other, or really to
us. They are more like voices in a Dantesque, infernal

13

space, where they cry out, relive their unforgettable moments, and see strange hallucinations.

The clue to their drama is in the epigraph which Eliot carefully positioned at the head of the poem. This is worth a word or two. It is a quotation from a Roman novel written in the time of the Emperor Nero and depicting the life and manners which prevailed during that most depraved phase of the Empire's decline. The quoted sentence refers to the Sybil of Cumae.

The Sybil was a not too distant Roman relative of the old Celtic *fili* – she was a seeress, the priestess of an oracle, the mouthpiece of truths and meanings from a divine source. And in former times the oracle at Cumae had been one of the most revered in the Roman world. Translated, the epigraph reads: 'And I saw with my own eyes the Sybil of Cumae hanging in a cage. And when boys shouted at her: "Sybil, what do you want?" she would answer: "I want only to die!" '

This Sybil, unable to escape from an existence that has become hideous, meaningless and hateful, is the link between all the women whose voices we hear, and whose doings we hear about, through the poem. As Eliot himself noted, all these women in the poem are one woman. And inevitably, because she is what she is, a holy woman, this Sybil also signifies that part of the soul, that power in the soul, which was formerly inspired and filled with true meaning from a divine source. Insofar as the Sybil is the essential female in the poem, we can hear *The Waste Land* as a love poem, an agonized love lament over what has happened to the sacred feminine source of love, and of existence itself in the modern world. Insofar as the Sybil is the soul, we can hear it as a religious poem, a testament of spiritual horror and despair.

The most important figure in the poem, as Eliot's note informs us, is one Tiresias. Tiresias, the most celebrated seer of the ancient classical world, the blind seer who had lived the lives of both a woman and a man. Insofar as the male and female voices of the poem meet (and Eliot specifically notes that they do) in Tiresias – insofar, that is, as Tiresias is the consciousness within which all the events of the poem occur – we can hear the poem as a kind of tragedy, a dramatization of the dark night of the soul, precipitated by a degradation of existence which was itself precipitated by a loss of contact with the divine source and a loss of all the meaning which the divine source gave.

The external shape of the poem gradually pieces itself together as a ritual – of death and rebirth. This is the central event of the Christian story, as it is the central mystical event of all the archaic Western religious cults from which Christianity emerged to create our civilization. Death of the seed, rebirth of the plant. Death of the body, resurrection of the soul. Death of the old soul, rebirth of the new soul. But the final context of the poem is not Christian or even Western.

There are many bizarre noises in *The Waste Land*: voices of water, speech of birds, and a jostling of fragments of other languages. But the unfamiliar language which finally embraces and enfolds all the voices and gathers up the whole poem is that of the Upanishads – the Sanskrit of those superhuman, ancient Hindu scriptures from which emerged Buddhism. It enters the poem as the voice of the Thunder, like the voice of the Creator, with three great words:

> Datta   Dayadhvam   Damyata

meaning

> Give   Sympathize   Control

These words approach, through the last section of the poem, spaced at intervals like the steps of the thunder-

storm bringing rain to the purgatorial Waste Land where
the voices are condemned to burn. The poem is brought
finally to a close with a fourth word, thrice repeated:

Shantih   Shantih   Shantih

This is the ending of an Upanishad. *Shantih* means,
approximately, 'The Peace which passes human understanding'. And the triple repetition, in the full phrase, has
been translated (by W. B. Yeats) as 'May Peace and
Peace and Peace be everywhere'.

As a final blessing, this evocation of the limits and
perimeter of human awareness, in the terms of a great
ascetic religion, can seem precarious. Little more,
perhaps, than a frail, containing sphere. Inside it, all the
anguished voices of the poem carry on as ever, reliving
their torments and the particularity of their lives, within
this extraordinary and wonderful work, exactly as in a
musical composition, and only waiting for us to hear
them.

3 · A DANCER TO GOD

A Toast to T. S. Eliot,
of which an abbreviated version
was delivered at the centenary dinner,
on 26 September 1988

I am sure we can all be agreed on one thing, on just how privileged we are to be here tonight as Valerie's guests.

Another way of putting it might be to say how keenly aware we all are, at this moment, of our privilege in having lived during the lifetime of Thomas Stearns Eliot, and in having found ourselves so close to him, in devotion, admiration and affection, that tonight we find ourselves here among Valerie's guests.

At a hundredth birthday I hope I can say that I am still youngish. But old enough, even so, to have grown accustomed to the tectonic shifts and readjustments in the literary and academic continents, as each new generation adapts itself to the Eliot vision and voice – to his continually growing presence. Those efforts of accommodation and understanding are part of a natural, historic process. But even where their public worth is slight, they can still be grateful, personal offerings. And tonight I would like to add to them with a small observation of my own.

A toast may be enough like a sermon to require a text. The text I have chosen for this evening is a very ancient one: the voice of Poetry as the voice of Eros.

I know our Master distinguished at least three voices of Poetry. Without questioning what he had to say about those, I would like to float a tentative hypothesis, a sort of unified field theory, and ask how far it can be applied to his own poetry.

First of all, I need to recruit the traditional idea of the poetic Self – that other voice which in the earliest times came to the poet as a god, took possession of him, delivered the poem, then left him. Or it came as the Muse, after the poet's prayers for her favour. Shakespeare only half mocked it as 'that affable familiar ghost' which nightly gulled his rival with intelligence. For Blake, it was the 'authors in eternity'. For the young Yeats, 'a clear articulation in the air'.

This familiar concept is worth a closer look. The qualifications of the poetic Self (apart from its inspiration) were: that it lived its own life separate from and for the most part hidden from the poet's ordinary personality; that it was not under his control, either in when it came and went or in what it said; and that it was supernatural. The most significant of these peculiarities was that it was supernatural. In ways that were sometimes less explicit than others, it emerged from and was merged with a metaphysical Universe centred on God. And it did this happily throughout history, right up to the beginning of this century.

I want to draw attention to what happened when this poetic Self mutated, as it so notoriously did. Imagine if Eliot, like Yeats, had heard that 'clear articulation in the air'. He might have been very glad of the lines, but he would have found no difficulty in recognizing the voice as an audial hallucination, in attributing it to a source located in his own subconscious mind, and in describing it as such to others.

Between the two men, born only twenty-three years apart, the shadow had fallen. It was human consciousness, we now see, and not simply the poetic Self, that had mutated. The undertow of Eliot's early tortured self-examination was the knowledge that this had irreversibly happened, that religious institutions and rituals had ceased to be real in the old sense, and that they continued to exist only as forms of 'make-believe', ways of behaviour rather than of belief. A new kind of reality had supplanted them. In the twinkling of an eye, as Nostradamus would say, the whole metaphysical universe centred on God had vanished from its place. It had evaporated, with all its meanings.

This emptiness was Eliot's starting-point. What seems curious was the suddenness of it. The historical convulsions leading up to it could be and were read as either death-struggles or birth-throes, and obviously they were both. But in spite of all those clear prophecies and ominous preparations, the actual birth, the final switch-over from amniotic ocean of buoyant soul to free-fall gulf of elemental oxygen, came as a stupefying shock, and with anything but a whimper, when the First World War left the truth bare. It was as if only now, at this moment, mankind was finally born. For the first time in his delusive history he had lost the supernatural world. He had lost the special terrors and cruelties of it, but also the infinite consolation, and the infinite inner riches. In its place he had found merely a new terror: the meaningless.

We see now that Eliot was the poet who brought the full implication of that moment into consciousness. It formed the features of his genius. It determined the novelty and scope and import of his greatness. And it decided his unique position in the history of poetry. That desacralized landscape had never been seen before. Or if it had been glimpsed, it had never before been real. Eliot found it, explored it, revealed it, gave it a name and a human voice. And almost immediately, everybody recognized it as their own.

It is natural to ask: what was it about him that so fitted him for the part? Because it is strange that, though so many other poets shared something of his awareness, no other actually embodied the vision and lived it, and articulated what that meant, as if the inescapable truths of it were inborn, as he did.

Perhaps it casts some preliminary light on Eliot to deflect the question slightly, and ask how this over-whelming desacralization of the Western World affected Yeats. Looking at him obliquely, and surveying only the bolder contours of his life and work, most readers would say that the distinguishing peculiarity of Yeats, among poets, lay in his preoccupation with the supernatural. Even to his earliest contemporaries this seemed already anachronistic, and as time passed it began to look even sillier: at best a wilful indulgence, at worst a little bit crazy, and, by any light, evidence of his fundamental lack of seriousness. To this day, when it is no longer done to doubt his seriousness, his appetite for the occult, for spirits, fairies and the ancient demi-gods, seems to many of his admirers incomprehensible, an eccentric, mistaken search for a system that might have been better supplied by something that all others understand or share, as indeed it did to Eliot. From Yeats's point of view, obvi-ously, it was anything but eccentric. He never really abandoned his early resolution, to make the work of poetry his first concern, the world of magic his second. And by magic as we know he did mean the real thing: arduous negotiation with spirits; regular, systematic, ritual dealings with the supernatural and supersensible realms. For him, the methodical work of magic had the kind of importance that accurate nuclear physics had for the makers of the Bomb: it was the path, as he saw it, towards the effective, practical fulfilment of his purpose – a life-work which he dedicated, quite consciously, to the service of his idea of Ireland.

One might well ask what instinct drew him to the supernatural in the first place. But the questions amplify hugely when one observes how every step and circum-

stance of his embattled life seems to have fed his spiritual
energy and reinforced his spiritual priorities. And when
one observes, too, just how effective and positive and
many were the parts that this occult energy enabled him
to play. It is certainly too simple to say what must have
been partly true, that his powers increased in proportion
to the determination with which he opposed, magician's
sword in hand, the ungovernable tides of secular mater-
ialism, especially the tide from England, as if that daily
labour served as some kind of gymnasium for a freakish
one-man religious system.

Part of Yeats's pattern comes a little clearer, perhaps,
when we set him in an anthropological context. It is fairly
easy then to recognize him as a shamanic type. The
classic moment for the advent of the messianic shaman,
the Saviour, arrives, as history repeatedly shows, where
the material hopes and resources of a people truly do
fail, and the desperate appeal to the miracle of spirit is
incarnated, to a greater or lesser degree, in some abnormal individual. The sense of tribal disaster that animated
Yeats was certainly compounded by shock waves from
Nietzsche, Darwin and other epicentres, but the decisive
event, imprinted on the face and voice of his every
fellow-countryman as in the Irish landscape itself, would
be that prolonged, genocidal humiliation where the Great
Famine and the mass emigrations that resulted from it,
falling across the childhood of his parents, were subjec-
tively experienced by all who felt themselves to be Irish as
the ultimate defeat, the bitter culmination of seven centuries of British policy in Ireland.

Yeats's calling came to him, in a sudden awakening, as
three simultaneous obsessions. Irish nationalist politics
and the supernatural possessed his intellectual life, while
Irish myth, legend and folklore took hold of his poetry.
He donned his spiritual breastplate of hermetic disciplines and within a very short time had formulated his

life mission on the grandest scale: to restore the energy and defiance of the ancestral heroes and lost gods to the prostrated soul of Ireland. This was pure shamanic thinking of the most primitive brand. It was closer to the visions of the Sioux Shaman Black Elk than to anything in the political or even poetic traditions of Western Europe. Throughout his labours as a political activist, Yeats's inspiration remained shamanic: to remake 'the ring of the people', to restore heroic, spiritual unity to his nation. His outspoken political statements all glow at some point into a shamanic flame, a sort of St Elmo's fire: where the enemy seemed about to triumph, eternity would put forth flaming fingers and bring their work to nothing; the moment before Ireland's destiny foundered on the rocks, a flaming hand would be laid upon the tiller. No matter how he was battered, as he was , by sharp-cornered modern realities, through all the tossings of his combative existence he swerved from his 'boyish plan', as he proclaimed exultantly, 'in nought'. He emerged into every new phase with his militant spirituality more joyful and tougher than ever. His political effectuality has been ridiculed by those who ridiculed the mysteries of spirit in which he put such faith, but after his lifelong campaign, fought stubbornly and exclusively from the nimble vantage of a first-century battle-chariot, Yeats thought it no accident when his own image of his poetic self, the warrior-saviour Cuchulain, materialized in bronze inside the O'Connell Street Post Office.

Surveyed in the same context, in the same broad way, and in comparison with Yeats, Eliot too looks not a little shamanic. In nervous temperament, and in the known psychological events of his late adolescence and early manhood, he is an even more extreme and characteristic example of the type than Yeats. But in him, the process of becoming aware of his calling was somehow more problematic. It was more agonized and finally more awe-

24

some. For one thing, through the whole, first, most vulnerable phase of it, he lacked any formal, or – as Yeats would have put it – magical defence. He survived and went forward on pure, naked character. The tribal disaster, in his case, was presumably just that convulsive desacralization of the spirit of the West. His tribe, perhaps, included all Western man, or perhaps, even, simply spiritual man. His homeland, in this sense, was that 'infinitely gentle, infinitely suffering' thing's hold on the nature of reality, and on the nature of consciousness, in a universe that had, in primitive fashion, lost its soul. But his response to the calamity was, maybe by the very nature of the calamity, which isolated the victims, more individualized than Yeats's, more remorselessly focussed within the wounds and exigencies of his own secret being. So it can seem to be a more crucial, a more surgically precise, more urgently human endeavour, being more privately personal at the one extreme and more universally public at the other. This appears in the difference between Yeats's heroic but untranslatably Irish Cuchulain and the universal, almost biological entity that emerged from the gulf to perform Eliot's inner drama.

Eliot's first consciousness of his task evolved from his attempts to deal with his sense of inner devastation, his perception of just how this general spiritual catastrophe had maimed and paralysed him, and of how this injury emptied life and the world of meaning. It is enlightening to watch his precocious intellectual skill bringing him to dead end after dead end, as he struggled to understand this condition in the very terms of the secular intelligence that had created it. And when his poetry opened a way, very briefly, during his impulsive experiment in Paris, where he put together *The Love Song of J. Alfred Prufrock*, he did not know how to take it. Perhaps he felt the time too soon and his hands too weak. He recoiled to the other extreme, into his determined attempt to adapt himself to a career in academic philosophy. At this point the summons to his real work rose before him in a significant form. At the time, he did not recognize it as a serious call. He acknowledged it as a disturbing, recurrent fascination, even an obsession. From this distance we can see that it was the old-fashioned thing: a religious vision. A half-primitive, nightmarish figure: the image of St Sebastian, a naked holy man, bound to a stake and pierced by many arrows. Outwardly, at least, it seemed to be St Sebastian. But Eliot himself wasn't so sure.

Who was it? What was it? Among other things it was proof, perhaps, that Eliot was able to contain within himself, more fully than any of his contemporaries, none of whom invented anything like it in inclusive complexity, depth and power, the spiritual tragedy of his epoch – of which this was an image, as it was in a more specific way of his own immediate psychological plight. Within this icon, that ascendant spirit of totalitarian, secular control – sceptical, scientific, steeled, flexible, rational, critical – displays its victim, the most profoundly aware and electrified plasm of the martyred psychosoma.

We see now more clearly the annunciation that stood behind Prufrock. However disparagingly Eliot tinkered with the various forms he tried to give it, this enigmatic vision effectively stopped him in his tracks. Even in his first explorations, it drew him out of his intellectual ego, out of his world of space and time, away from the academic temptation and into its own peculiar agony.

We have no problem nowadays in seeing that the God-centred metaphysical universe of the religions suffered not so much an evaporation as a translocation. It was interiorized. And translated. We live in the translation, where what had been religious and centred on God is psychological and centred on an idea of the self – albeit a self that remains a measureless if not infinite question mark.

Before the translation became a near-universal myth-ology, there was a draughty interim. It seemed as though the poetic enterprise might be over. Even in the 1940s and 1950s it was common to hear poets lamenting the futility, the irrelevance and above all the obsolescence of their art in the modern world. It is perhaps not so much an irony as a piece of evolution's natural economy that the little mechanism of free-association, which Freud picked up indirectly from Schiller, who used it to unblock his creative flow, should have been the means of disman-tling the old-style mystery of poetic inspiration and the poetic self – or rather, of translating them.

In the end, of course, nothing disrupted the basic arrangements. The translation was first class. An ordinary ego still has to sleep and wake with some other more or less articulate personality hidden inside it, or behind it or beneath it, who carries on, just as before, living its own outlandish life, and who turns out, in fact, to be very like the old poetic self: secularized, privatized, maybe only rarely poetic, but recognizably the same, autonomous, mostly incommunicado, keeper of the dreams. Psycho-analysis simply re-drafted the co-tenancy contract in the new language. But in the process it did slightly change some things. By shifting the emphasis of certain clauses, it confirmed this other self, this new-style possibly poetic self, in powers that had previously often been challenged. It ensured, for instance, that this *doppelgänger*, though it might remain much of the time incognito, will always be dominant, with its hands, one way or another, on the controls; it will always possess superior knowledge about what is happening and will happen to the creature in which it dwells; and, more important, and reintroducing with a bang the heady higher gyroscope of a sacred creation, it may represent and may even contain, in its vital and so to speak genetic nucleus, the true self, the self at the source, that inmost core of the individual,

which the Upanishads call the divine self, the most inac-
cessible thing of all.

But more important still, psychoanalysis re-established,
as its first principle, the ancient and formerly divine first
law of psychodynamics, which states: any communion
with that other personality, especially when it does incor-
porate some form of the true self, is healing, and
redeems the sufferings of life, and releases joy. In this
respect, at least, the new and desacralized world has
ended up very close to the most archaic and spiritualized,
where poetry from the true source was acknowledged to
be divine because it heals, and redeems the sufferings of
life, and releases joy. As if it secreted, in some drug-like
essence, the ungainsayable reassurance of the Creator
himself.

There is one further well-worked law, fundamental to
psychoanalysis and to the modern secular outlook, which
I would like to move to the centre of my remarks tonight.
This concerns the inevitability with which the true self,
once it is awakened, and no matter how deeply and
silently buried in the bones it may be, will always try to
become the conscious centre of the whole being.

If we specify a poet in whom the poetic self is indeed,
in this way, the true self, then the translation from old-
style poetic self to new-style has left virtually everything
intact, except the climate of expectation and possibility in
which his readers live. And this very rough identification
holds good, I believe, for Eliot. He is, in fact, an exemplary case. In his poetry all the characteristics of the new-
style poetic self are apparent, present in the fullest
possible strength, without obscuration or dilution, and
my comments tonight really concern only him.

The translation has changed one or two things for the
poet. It has also sharpened our awareness of what is
actually going on in his work. It has changed things for
the poet by removing his susceptibility to the trance

condition, the mood in which the poetic self could over-power the whole mind in a more unhindered fashion. That this susceptibility has gone is a fact. There are some obvious psychological reasons for its demise, all connected with the loss of instinctive self-subjection to the greater authority of spirit. As Goethe remarked, the necessary trance is the most fragile piece of the poet's equipment. The mere presence of another person in the same house was enough to destroy his. But the pervasive-ness of secular scepticism operates generally. Even Bali-nese dancers, trained from childhood to enter the trance in which their movements can happen, utterly lose the ability after quite a short dip into Western attitudes. For any poet, this loss means acute distress. It means, in effect, that the poetic self's bid to convert the ordinary personality to its own terms, or to supplant it, or to dissolve it within itself, will be more successfully resisted. And this in turn means depression – the unproductive poet's melancholia. Or it may take the form of violent psychological or even physical breakdown, or religious crisis. A stealthier osmosis, in modern times, requires exceptional disciplines of monastic self-surrender – evi-dently. Again, Eliot is almost the only example among modern poets to suggest that this might be one possible way to complete the inner process.

He underwent both the depression and the violent collapse of ego. The ordeal of parturition, from which *The Waste Land* emerged, marks at least one occasion where his ordinary personality had to be forcibly dis-placed, before that other speech and that other life, his true speech and life, could be spoken and lived even temporarily. He underwent the religious crisis, in circum-stances that seem to have been only less openly painful. And as I hope to show, he submitted himself, in his private meditation and poetic work ('humility is endless') to the slow, gradual change, according to that pattern where the true self remakes the ego in its own image, till the individual is wholly transformed, and the true self takes over, as openly as may be, the activities and satisfactions of life in the world.

The details support these generalities. Because in each case the make-up of the poetic self is so unique, its idiosyncrasies have consequences that are as peculiar as they are fateful. The new translation has sharpened our eyes to observe this. The poet's each successive creation can be read as the poetic self's effort to make itself known, to further its takeover. This effort embodies itself in a complete visionary symbol of the poetic self and its separated predicament. The distinguishing features of this kind of image are just those – that it is visionary, that it is irreducibly symbolic, and that it is dramatically complete.

The successive visions evolve in time according to the way the poetic self evolves in its hidden life. But in the series which make up the poet's opus, the earliest are often the most revealing, either because the interfering ego is weakest then, or because these creative visions are very like conventional serial dreams, in that the first successful representation is likely to be a compact index of everything to follow. The final poetic object is inevitably a mongrel, a record of the conflict of selves, partly what the limited, vigilant, personal ego has made of an ultimately unfathomable vision, partly what the vision has made of the inadequate ego, and partly the result of the contractual labours of a go-between or mediator, that third entity who argues both sides, or curses both sides, or despairs between them, or is torn apart by them, or successfully makes – on some terms or other – peace. But the ego might have good cause to resist. When the true self, for all its supremacy, happens to be deadlocked with some fatal disease or psychic death-sentence, and the conclusion is foregone, the knowledge will be there in the emerging image of the self's declaration.

The image that Keats found was of this sort: *Endymion*, 'La Belle Dame Sans Merci', 'The Pot of Basil', 'Lamia', are complete images of the poetic self locked in a death-struggle, and predict the fate that took Keats with it. Coleridge's vision of *The Ancient Mariner* is another, also ominous, though with a saving difference, in that it prophesied a metaphysical death to the poetic self – but to the ordinary ego a long posthumous life telling the metaphysical tale. This illustrates what I mean by the 'fateful' quality of this kind of image. It can be just as surely so where the prognosis, as in Eliot's case, is harrowing – but ultimately good.

All this is a great simplification, besides being well known, but I have taken a detour through it because it clarifies my main point, and assembles the precedents, the relevant ones, for an answer to the question with which I began, where I asked, to change the wording slightly, what link is there between Eliot's poetry and that seminal deity of the ancient world – Eros, the god of love?

Nowadays Eros is a fluid term, coursing through all the familiar biological effects. Formerly, too, he had many names, faces, biographies. For the scope of my speculations tonight, I want to define him more narrowly.

But my first step, not at all a digression, is another question: what is the real name of that quasi-divine figure who appears in Eliot's unforgettable early poem, *The Death of St Narcissus?* Here is the whole poem:

The Death of Saint Narcissus

Come under the shadow of this gray rock –
Come in under the shadow of this gray rock,
And I will show you something different from either

Your shadow sprawling over the sand at daybreak, or
Your shadow leaping behind the fire against the red rock:
I will show you his bloody cloth and limbs
And the gray shadow on his lips.

    He walked once between the sea and the high cliffs
When the wind made him aware of his limbs smoothly
       passing each other
And of his arms crossed over his breast.
When he walked over the meadows
He was stifled and soothed by his own rhythm.
By the river
His eyes were aware of the pointed corners of his eyes
And his hands aware of the pointed tips of his fingers.

Struck down by such knowledge
He could not live men's ways, but became a dancer
       before God
If he walked in city streets
He seemed to tread on faces, convulsive thighs and
       knees.
So he came out under the rock.

    First he was sure that he had been a tree,
Twisting its branches among each other
And tangling its roots among each other.

    Then he knew that he had been a fish
With slippery white belly held tight in his own fingers,
Writhing in his own clutch, his ancient beauty
Caught fast in the pink tips of his new beauty.

    Then he had been a young girl
Caught in the woods by a drunken old man
Knowing at the end the taste of his own whiteness
The horror of his own smoothness,
And he felt drunken and old.

So he became a dancer to God.
Because his flesh was in love with the burning arrows
He danced on the hot sand
Until the arrows came.
As he embraced them his white skin surrendered itself to
    the redness of blood, and satisfied him.
Now he is green, dry and stained
With the shadow in his mouth.

If we grant this mysterious being respectable status, and call him one of Eliot's earliest and most strikingly successful 'objective correlatives', and one moreover of compelling visionary impact, we can then ask, still using his own terms, what 'dark embryo' does it deliver to the light?

Before we try to answer we might just check that the poem does stand very oddly alone, in an odd position, at the threshold of the *Collected Poems* yet not within. Outside the mature work, there is nothing remotely like it – except the fantasia of *St Sebastian*, which serves, rather, like an aborted twin, to intensify the survivor's uniqueness. Yet within the *Collected Poems* almost every poem, certainly every major poem, seems related to it in some uterine fashion.

Eliot seems to have liked it. He evidently considered letting Pound publish it, and though he thought better of that he did acknowledge the poem's membership of the family when he implanted key lines from it into *The Waste Land* – where again they became key lines. In retrospect, *The Waste Land* can look like the full-term accouchement where this *Death of St Narcissus* would be a surgical colour slide of an early stage of the foetus. In a similar way, the major poems which follow it as if they had grown out of it, persuade us to accept this work – for all its germinal, raw tenderness – as the first portrait, perhaps the only full-face portrait, of Eliot's genius.

The next conjectural step, in consolidation of that last remark, is quite a large one. Does this poem present an image of Eliot's poetic self? For tonight, I accept that it does exactly this. I ask you to believe that the poem records the moment when, looking into the pool beneath his ordinary personality, Eliot's poetic self caught a moment of tranced stillness, and became very precisely aware of its own peculiar nature, inheritance and fate, and found for itself this image.

Can a single early poem carry so much responsibility, even when we allow for what we know of Eliot's obsessive interest in the theme? Among his published early poems one other piece presents a very recognizable Eliot persona which might be thought just as likely a candidate for the role of the poetic Self's image. This is *Humouresque*, Eliot's lament for his dead marionette.*

The two poems complement each other. The marionette is another form of the early Eliot's familiar Laforgue dandy of wittily rhyming, ironic self-deprecation. He is a failed larval variant of the rueful Prufrockian self-parody who feels himself inadequate not only to the appeals of love and life, but to a whole flashing cloudful of higher demands. He is no St Narcissus. Yet there is something of St Narcissus about him: he shares that curious neurasthenic self-awareness of himself as a thing, a puppet on strings. But while St Narcissus consecrates in a dance his horror of his own beauty, this marionette burlesques the pathetic ugliness of his own emptiness. He is Eliot's parody of the ego who longs to be that other, even as he excuses himself from the unmanageable confrontation; the self who is, one way and another, no more than a shadow of what he dissociates himself from so regretfully. He is the fatally-drained obverse of St Narcissus, striving to construct and maintain a brittly correct face for the outer world, while the entire life of his organism has

*See note, p. 53.

34

been sucked up into that burning, sacred but far-removed and fugitive existence of the poetic self, that self-abandoned, anachronistic 'dancer to God', St Narcissus, who lives in a language as unlike that of Laforgue as possible, a language saturated with that of Holy Scripture, as he suffers and bleeds his way into the ultimate life of a death in God.

So even *Humouresque* redirects us to St Narcissus as the accurate, real, sensitive portrait of the original poetic self, just as surely as the later poems point back to these two figures to confirm their contrapuntal roles.

However we look at it, 'The Death of Saint Narcissus' is far from slight. The actuality of this dancing aboriginal is weirdly disturbing. And the visionary definition, the deep-focus radiance of the scene, is uncanny. His balletic, orgiastic sanctity suggests the presence of the true self in an unveiled form, and something more too, something like Blake's 'fury of a spiritual existence'. Remembering Coleridge's Mariner and Keats's La Belle Dame, and thinking ahead through Eliot's future, we look again at this protagonist. We wonder what the implications might be.

The name St Narcissus is pointedly compounded and odd. It stirs up a welter of premonitory signals – the drowned self, the female, disembodied, crying voice – from the fable of Narcissus, but at the same time fixes primarily that aspect of the image as a mirrored reflection. While the poem opens the holy figure to a tangle of origins that are simultaneously primeval, far back in organic life, primitive and classical, the name pins him to a martyred Christian future. Though it sets him historically in the second century, as a former Bishop of Jerusalem, it makes an emblem of him and embeds him in the mythic, hieratic light of the mystery religions, where the earliest, ecstatic mystai in the caves and the last Gnostic frenzies in the desert dance the one dance. In this last role he reveals an even more specific history.

35

Painted on a tomb wall, he would have to be identified as some form of Eros/Dionysus, the androgynous, protean daemon of biological existence and the reproductive cycle. He remembers his other lives: as a young girl, a fish, a tree. He has lived (and still lives) the sexual life of both female and male; he is the god who was (and is) a fish; he is the god in the tree. He is the god who 'could not live man's ways' and who, as the elemental and timeless incarnation of all the dying gods of the birth, copulation and death mythos – Thammuz, Attis, Osiris and the rest – was one way or another torn to pieces, mourned for and reborn: the god who was finally assumed as the tragic, sacrificed form of Eros, simply the god of love. In this way, the poem openly reclaims the sanctity of biological and primitive feeling, and fuses it with a covert, Loyolan variant of the life and death of Christ.

Having said that, what gives a reader pause is maybe what prompted Eliot to withdraw the poem from publication. Whether it is too gauche or too bold in its intimate self-revelation, almost its self-exposure, is difficult to say. The physical details and the subjective feeling attached to them are experienced with such first-hand intensity they reduce the mythic/historic context to nothing more than a theatre backdrop, while this dance in the foreground is suffered through like a biological transformation, so nakedly that it is shocking – holy but shocking, in the way that an axolotl held writhing in the fingers, or a squirming, bared foetus might be said to be holy but shocking. As the image moves it transmits a high-voltage *frisson*, a sort of alternating current of voluptuous horror and mystical rapture: a supercharge, one might say, of the richest erotic feeling going through a very bizarre transmutation.

If this is an 'objective correlative' for Eliot's poetic Self, what are the implications, the consequences, for

36

him? Setting aside the Ancient Mariner and La Belle
Dame, and giving only a steadying glance towards the
more startling but maybe more comparable example of
Nietzsche's vision encounter with Wotan, we could fix
our attention, first of all, on the fact that the mirror
image of Eliot's poetic Self is a god, and not only a god
but (albeit in disguise) the supreme autochthonous god of
the natural cycle and of the cultures of the West.

On the negative side, this suggests that the poet's
ordinary life will be pre-empted, that sacred responsibili-
ties will be imposed, whether he accepts them or not, and
that some heavy personal cost will be exacted.

Up to this point, Eliot's Eros bodes no better than
Nietzsche's Wotan. The similarity ends there. Wotan
enforced his programme on Nietzsche, and maybe that
was the human cost, exacted at the end, through those
last years. But Eros exacted his cost at the beginning.
Everything about Eliot's early life suggests that in some
obscure part of himself he had foresuffered the sacrificial
death of that deity even before he began to write under
compulsion. This event, which was so much of his
theme, and which lies so visibly among the roots of his
poetry, can be seen as the spontaneous occurrence, in
extraordinarily vivid and literal form, within him of that
universal phenomenon, the traditional shaman's crucial
initiatory experience of visionary dismemberment. And
just as only after that 'death' (and after being re-
assembled by divine beings) the conventional shaman can
begin to turn his abnormal powers and susceptibilities to
account and launch out on his poetic, dramatic, visionary,
healing-trance enterprise for the benefit of his people, so
Eliot's case suggests how closely the creative, redemptive
activity of poetry (of art in general) conforms to this
thaumaturgical, natural process: where the shaman
is possessed by the daemon of his own excess of
natural healing power, as if artistic creation were the

37

psychological component of the galvanized auto-immune system. After the sacrificial death, for Eliot, came the years of mourning. But before the end came rebirth.

Stopping short of the suggestion that the form of Eros alive and dead in Eliot's vision is also the daemon of the auto-immune system, we can see that for him the 'fateful' consequences wait within this particular deity's potential for suffering, for spiritual and moral recovery and growth, for universality, and for the most intimately human historical significance.

In other words, the 'bloody cloth and limbs' of St Narcissus lie at the root of the family tree of Western cultures. This doomed, epicene, immortal exquisite, dancing his archaic Aphrodisian/Dionysian role in the tree of nerves, anticipates, as Eliot depicts him, the greater part of Western spiritual developments till they coalesce, ultimately, into the person of Christ, and ramify through all the Christian values of our civilization. The whole achievement is innate in the secret, naked god. At the same time, even in so early a poem, Eliot holds all possible relationships carefully open, and certain attitudes of this shape-changer more than suggest a kinship with the blue-faced Hindu Krishna who performs, one way and another, the epiphany at the core of Buddhism, cognate with the divine self, 'that person in the heart, no bigger than a thumb, maker of past and future', the child in the lotus who 'beyond suffering suffers from life to life'. In this perspective, the holy manikin, so spookily alive in Eliot's poem, appears as a skeleton key to the spirituality of the East as well as the West.

I keep well in mind that I am talking about Eliot's concealed (and for the most part incomprehensible to him, too) inner life. No discussion of this can get much beyond hints followed by guesses. Even to the most flexible hypothesis St Narcissus can never be more than a symbol, a composite cryptogram, for what was actually living there in Eliot's hidden being; and the word 'divine', with its relatives, can never be more than a convenient finger-post pointing towards those orders of experience which mankind goes on stumbling into, in terror and awe, even while he argues about them in terms of brain rhythms and brain chemistry. But however we approach it, we have to accept that what was actually there, behind the symbol he found for it, was decisive. And this is the sense in which that early vision determined, at each crossroads, the unique route of his poetic adventure, the unusual kind of greatness he was able to achieve, and the altogether unprecedented, universal and near-papal authority in which his greatness finally came to rest. Even that epithet 'papal', used so often jokingly, chimes aptly back through all I have been saying.

This link between the form that Eros takes in his early poem, and what Eliot was able to accomplish in his poetic career, holds the kernel of my words tonight. As a hieroglyphic device, a genetic code, 'The Death of Saint Narcissus' is true to the event, but it cannot explain some things. It cannot explain Eliot's single-minded intensity, the tenacity with which he explored all that opened within and beyond that inner confrontation, nor the quality of the intellectual/moral gifts which enabled him to turn that inner exposure and opportunity to such prodigious account. It only tells us why, once the sufferings of Eros had emerged and constellated as the drama of his life, that direction of his inner evolution became inevitable. The theoretical alternative of inwardly disconnecting from the painful process and escaping into some kind of anaesthesia was as impossible for him as if by the failure of his self-protective nerve-chemistry. Where 'the ordinary wakeful life of the ego' was cut off from the spirit's search, he seems to have experienced it as a damnation, a bestial and mechanical horror, 'meaning Death'. Indeed, it was *The Waste Land*, the nightmare vision of the desacralized world, where the chosen Son of Man, opposing God, cursed by the prophets, stared from the protozoic slime, in a circle of meaningless reflexes.

As all observers agree, he was a bafflingly elusive and complicated being. His work and personality together present a maze of riddles. But the view I have proposed, which is no more than a tendered appraisal of the double existence forced on to him by his strangely masterful other self, makes it possible to see several features of his life and work in a fairly coherent pattern.

It throws some light, of a kind, on what one might call the biology of certain extreme attitudes evident in his personality and his prose. It illuminates, for instance, what he meant by the word 'impersonality', and by his insistence on the clean division between the poetry and the man, and why, for him, such precautions were so fundamental. And perhaps that special urgency, the psychological acuteness and depth of his critical intelligence, drew more than a little of its curious authority from the inner disciplines which were, in his case, survival techniques, by which he simultaneously protected his inner world of precarious gestations and sacred events, and yet maintained a sceptical, vigilant distance from what were by ordinary standards its impossible, supernatural demands, while at the same time he negotiated with it in a perpetual 'summit' crisis effort to make meaningful sense of it and to come to terms with it.

Consideration of this life of double-exposure helps, too, in any understanding of what was, maybe, almost an occult ingredient in the maelstrom disturbances that beset him. But most concretely of all, it throws into relief a pattern of completeness and inevitability behind the poems.

The quality that we feel to be his 'greatness' is there in each passage of the verse, and usually in each line. But even in these minutiae of verbal tone, cadence and texture, it is 'greatness' of a densely characteristic and consistently blended sort. The notable distinction of it is that it stands slightly outside, a reader sets it automatically slightly outside, what we think of as the 'literary'. To compare it in this respect with the work of any other poet in English throws this peculiarity into relief. In all his poems up to the end of *Ash Wednesday* the poetry lacks that provisional air of 'licence', a sense of liberties taken, such as pervades even the most solemn moments of any other major poet. Usually this licence, of word, metaphor or whatever, is the very wings of their flight, the masterful resource that lifts them over gulfs. Contingent struggle, expedient means, exuberant freedom from all sacred control, the fluidity of improvised solutions, for almost all poets these are the stuff of invention. Eliot eschews them utterly. His near-uniqueness in this particular appears even more sharply in the relationship between his poetry and certain passages of the King James Bible. Even such a comparatively profane book as *The Song of Songs*, in that translation, gives no sense of 'provisional licence'. If Shakespeare, Milton, Blake, Wordsworth, others, were to replace any chapter of that with a piece of their own characteristic verse, though each might produce a masterpiece, we can see that the most important thing would be lost. The sacred inevitability, that radiant, incantatory wholeness and finality, which is the glory of the King James translation, is a language inspired by profound, unbroken mythical/religious feeling, untainted by literary motive or secular fantasy, and presented as an offering to God, if within hearing of man. One can feel behind the wording of each verse the impersonal seriousness of a holy purpose deepened and accumulated through centuries. In this sense, the translators were not composing a literary work, and the results remain outside 'literature'. Eliot strove to reconnect his feeling and, on the evidence of it, his motivation too, to those of the King James translators, so we might expect the ghost of their solidarity to lift his words a little outside 'literature', as indeed it did, more and more noticeably as his faith consolidated itself. But these efforts were merely part of his deliberate attempt to open himself to that other ghost, the god within St Narcissus, that consanguineous voice which had spoken to him at his beginning.

The Song of Songs could be (we are told it well might have been) a text from some part of a ritual oratorio concerning an Eros/Thammuz or similar deity. And so the pierced god, the incantatory flight, the sensual/mystical exaltation, those integral components of Eliot's affliction, brought him closer, in a secret, proprietorial sense, to *The Song of Songs*, than any translator. Maybe this was his umbilical link to biblical poetry in general, as to the language and authority of a prophet of the sacred values. If the two main currents of power in *The Song of Songs* are erotic feeling and mystical adoration, a sustained ground bass of overwhelming erotic feeling mingling with what might be called a higher harmonic of mystical, self-sacrificial adoration, it is exactly this combination which oscillates from one pole to the other in 'The Death of Saint Narcissus', and which rises to those moments in 'La Figlia Che Piange', in the hyacinth girl passage in *The Waste Land*, and in parts of *Ash Wednesday*, providing the surge for those highest peaks in the love poetry of the language. We feel the same amalgam throughout his poetry – it is the musical body of the voice; but apart from these almost pure moments we hear it everywhere suffering, embroiled with the anguished complexities of that severe puritan ego, in swarming variation of pain and sublimation, the mutilated sacrament which the god's tragedy is in any world but particularly here in this modern one, and which stamps the substance of each line. Or if not of absolutely every line, certainly of every juxtaposed pair of lines. The electrical charge and

transmission of that drama at the centre delivers its
coded signal at every point in the whole magnetic field.
But it is in Eliot's successful, artistic projection of this
whole drama that his full greatness reveals itself.

Considered as a drama, with a beginning, middle and
end, his poems recapitulate the historical evolution of the
deity from the earliest primal form of Eros to the incarnation worshipped by a modern mystical Anglo-Catholic.
At the same time, and in the same terms, they recapitulate the psychological process which moves from the
death (in whatever circumstances) of primitive Eros in
the psychosomatic order, through that alchemy of mourning, to the rebirth of Love as a Christ figure in the
spiritual order. Phylogony and ontogeny of the entire
metamorphosis cohere, in the richest and densest way, in
the organic development of the *Collected Poems*.

The unfolding of the action can be followed poem by
poem. The advent of the divinity, the Love-god, passes
(after Prufrock, the diffident John the Baptist, who
deplores his own incapacity to acknowledge let alone
evangelize for the god whose death he has already in
some way foresuffered) through the sacrificial dismemberment and scattering of the parts. This death is the
psychic devastation behind the limbo of *The Waste Land*.
The dark night of the fragments scattered and crying lies
behind *The Hollow Men*. In a harrowing rebirth, out of
the nadir, the Christ soul emerges, surrounded by 'Jour-
ney of the Magi', 'Animula', 'Marina', 'A Song for
Simeon', each of which stands in an emergency relationship to its nativity. This new soul is a resurrection of all
the energies of Eros, but now refocused, within the
Christian ethos, in adoration of the supernatural woman
of *Ash Wednesday*, who brings him to submission before
God the Father. The final drama of his decision to reject
the world publicly and become a dancer to God (com-
pleting the life-plan laid down in 'The Death of Saint

Narcissus') rises through the parable of *Murder in the Cathedral* to the rose-window, many-petalled choreography of the dance before God in an English chapel, which is the pattern of the *Four Quartets*.

At that point the poetic Self and the ordinary personality, the Rose and the Fire, became one. In religious terms, the sufferings of the god and the sufferings of the ego were, as near as may be, united in a pattern of redemption. In poetic terms, his heroic, sacred drama was triumphantly completed. From dismemberment in the meaningless, he had rescued a spiritual wholeness, and reconstructed a new ground of rejoicing. And as he performed this feat he created, in his poetry, a ritual dramatic form which established that process as a real possibility for others. What had begun as a shamanic crisis-call to regeneration, in the depths of the adolescent, matriarchal psyche, a dark place of savage drumming which he referred to often enough but never tried to disown, drew him through those flames of the tragedy of Eros into an *imitatio Christi* and the paternal authority of a high priest in a world religion.

That Eliot undertook this task on such a large scale, and accomplished it in such terms, goes some way towards suggesting the true measure of his greatness. This is how his poetry comes to stand, as it seems to do, at the centre of revelation in this age, and, as poetry, to stand there alone.

My opening text was: the voice of poetry as the voice of Eros. If poetry is the voice of Eros, or, perhaps, the text of some fragment of the loves and sufferings of Eros, it might be argued, from what I have proposed, that Eliot is the purest of all poets, the most authentic of all poets. What other poet's work concerns itself so exclusively with, and presents so profoundly and passionately and completely, in all its human implication, the life and death in the flesh and the resurrection into spirit of that god? It is one more peculiarity about Eliot: he wrote virtually no occasional verse, or only so little as to remind us of its virtual absence, no discoursive verse of the secular ego – which makes up, after all, approximately 100 per cent of what the rest of the world writes. Where the sacred drama found no release, or could beam no refracted light, he simply wrote the very different language of his prose. And when the drama was completed – as no other poet in English ever did complete it – he was released from the labours. He had achieved a genuine happiness, symbolized and realized in his late marriage, united to his true self and to the world.

As I said at the beginning, I offer these remarks tonight as a tentative unified field theory. I fancy the substance of the theory can be seen – like a fish lying beneath a turbulent, swift but clear current – from a certain angle, at a certain slant of light. I have suspended scholarly disbelief, and adopted the attitude of an inter-pretative, performing musician. As he reads the score, the musician imagines he finds the living spirit of the music, the inmost vital being of a stranger, reproduced sponta-neously, inside himself. And so he describes his perform-ance in the style of programme notes, as an exploratory X-ray of processes within the dark embryo, though he knows perfectly well that even the most rigorous scholar-ship hardly hopes to get beyond its own space-flights of subjective phantasmagoria.

It would take an iron nerve to be more than tentative in this field. Each year Eliot's presence reasserts itself at a deeper level, to an audience that is surprised to find itself more chastened, more astonished, more humble, where the whole task of understanding can seem more and more like King Lear endlessly trying to fathom the unspeaking mystery of Cordelia.

Perhaps it has not been easy for our century to accept that Eliot is not merely a great poet, but a poet who stands in English with maybe only one other name; a poet, as I have tried to describe, of an utterly new species, who produced pages that prompt a reader to ask where their equals are to be found.

It is certain that I am not the only person to wonder what two or three pages exist, in world poetry, to set beside 'Gerontion', or the second part of *Ash Wednesday*. And as Pound said, where are the nineteen pages to stand beside *The Waste Land*? Or the thirty pages to stand with the *Four Quartets*? Even when we produce challengers, can we ever be certain about the judgement?

Much that I have said tonight, I'm afraid, would displease him. I imagine how appalled he would be by my application of the theology of Eros to his secret meditations. It might well confirm his feelings about centenaries. On the other hand, this is his birthday. And on what day is he more likely to be present, and in what place, than now and here, in L'Ecu de France? And particularly on this birthday, when his return to the living has taken such a long step, with the publication of the first volume of Valerie's edition of his letters. This is a substantial kind of rebirth. And Valerie's magnificent and meticulous labours are now an even greater part of his immortality than they were.

In paranormal research, it has been discovered that if everybody in the room assumes that a spirit is present and does indeed act as if the spirit were present, the spirit can make itself felt in most convincing ways. Without defining spirit too childishly, let us imagine him present.

And I ask you, ladies and gentlemen, to rise and join me in a salute to our invisible host, our master of masters, this very great poet among the very greatest, on his hundredth birthday; and the same salute must include

46

the woman who has never been separated from him, and who has devoted her life to his happiness and to his continuing presence and increasing authority in the world:

to THOMAS STEARNS ELIOT

NOTES

1 THE TRULY GREAT

After a long campaign, Mrs T. S. Eliot finally secured an
English Heritage blue name plaque for the wall outside
the apartment where T. S. Eliot had lived from 1957
until his death in 1965. I was invited to unveil the plaque
and say a few words. It was a sparkling sunny morning,
with occasional passers-by in the street, when I delivered
this short address, from the steps outside the apartment,
to the assembled guests.

I based my remarks about Eliot's international standing
among poets born in the early 1920s and earlier on what
I have heard from them personally. After hearing this
judgement advanced by two or three, I made a point, over
the years, of finding out what others felt about him. For
my own part, it was no difficulty to speak of him without
reservation.

2 THE SONG OF SONGS IN THE VALLEY OF BONES

This piece served a triple purpose. The occasion was a
fundraising event for the Arvon Writing Foundation,
organized by Josephine Hart, and dedicated to T. S. Eliot
on his centenary. The programme centred on a reading

of *The Waste Land*, and included lyrics by W. B. Yeats. My own role, as a spokesman for the Arvon Foundation, was to thank the benefactors and the audience, and to salute T. S. Eliot by way of a brief introduction to the recital of *The Waste Land*. In the time available, I limited myself to highlighting prominent structural features that might be useful to a listener.

3 A DANCER TO GOD

The centenary dinner for T. S. Eliot was given by Mrs Eliot at his favourite restaurant, L'Ecu de France in Jermyn Street, and coincided with the publication of the first volume of her edition of his letters.

This address seemed to me too compacted in its burrowing and perhaps at some points arcane argument, and also too long, to be delivered as a toast, in the form printed here. On the occasion, I delivered a shortened, simpler version.

Now even the original seems far too simple and impressionistic. Only a much fuller treatment, I think, could begin to substantiate my basic suggestion, in which I propose that Eliot the poet completed, with almost unique high definition and brilliance, the sacral, inner transformation of a certain type of sensibility, and that his poems are dramatic formulations of the distinctive phases through which this transformation must pass. It seems to me that only one other poet in the canon of English poetry is really comparable to him in this respect: the 'god' who confronted Eliot in his early days, disguised here as St Sebastian, and dramatized there in his 'juvenile' poem 'The Death of Saint Narcissus', was the same 'god' who appeared before Shakespeare when, at the age of twenty-eight or so, he summoned for the first time a purely poetic theme – and found himself dealing with the